K B A R P

Khaidji's **B**ajan **A**crostic **R**hyming **P**oetry

First Edition

Acrostic Poetry

Written by

Khaidji

ISBN 978-1-365-29158-6

ISBN 978-1-365-29158-6

Legal

Preface

One of the widest collections of acrostic poems anywhere it the world with unique perspective on fictional and non-fictional. Subjects that span varied regions with emphasis on things Barbadian.

The collection includes some highly specific poems designed to offer solace and support to the ailing and their care givers. It also contains traditional local jokes from Barbados where Khaidji adapts folk's jokes of local personality Ossie Moore and stretched them into short anecdotes in acrostic poetry. Read also the many poems of spiritual guidance and inspiration, and an array of other categories.

Acknowledgement

None of my work was possible without the inspiration from The Lord Jesus Christ, without whose guidance, graces and glory I was helpless.
The illness which retired me from my regular work also gave me a greater opportunity to use the talents the Lord has entrusted me.

I am eternally grateful to my immediate family and close friends who with their endless support, encouraged me to express myself and trust in the Lord's guidance.

And for all those who continued to say, publish Khaidji, thank you, I have!

Author's Profile

Khaidji (pronounced Kaygee or simply KG) has written over 4000 acrostic poems, many of which cover topics like the lead up to the American Presidential Nominations of 2008, superstar Rihanna, and many of the daily encounters with local and International news, religion and more.

Hidden Messages is the first of a series. Path to The White House is a chronicle of the lead up to the Presidency of the United States for Barack Obama. Khaidji is a wide commentator in the Blogosphere and has been read on local talk shows. The range of categories of Khaidji's writings is contracted for use in greetings cards, promotional materials, advertising and other commercial and creative ideas.

Titles to date

Hidden Messages
Path To The White House
Tender Moments Revealed
Beyond The Roots
I STARVE Daily
Rihanna - A Robyn Flying High
Views of the News
Turned On
The Mighty Spirit
The Air Wave
A Strike like ike
The Holy Joint
GoOD Day
My Alma Mater
BIM - Barbados Island Memories
Life Leif
KBARP

Table Of Contents

By Appearance

Table of Contents

by Category

A Eyeful en' A Bellyful

Apples and chocolate with marshmallows and strawberry

Enticing treats lying on the table were eye candy
Your eyes will see things and yearn for them
Eyeful is seeing, then yearning, then you're overwhelm'
Full from seeing and never getting a bite
Uneasy feelings that bring us joy but never delight
Looking on makes you want to savor the treat

Eye candy is only good when you're allowed to eat
Now the stomach is the way to a man's heart

A basket of eye candy and his cravings will start

But if taken away when his eyes are popping
Elevated hormones rush with little chance for stopping
Looking and not touching or eating these delicacies
Leaves men thinking that you were only a tease
You shouldn't give a man an eyeful and just
Forbid him from partaking and leave him to lust
Unfairly women may tempt then restrict and say a bit much
Like a eyeful en' a bellyful, yuh cuh see but doan touch

A Persona Non Grata

A lotta people does mek de same mistake

Putting up wid violence 'til we at dem wake
Especially de women wid insecurities
Rihanna, tell me, you 'aint one of dese
Sure, you may never had known before
Or you may had wanted to tame de young gully-boar
Nah more, not even if you weren't de one
A rap like dis, it's time tuh be long gone

Nevah stick 'round any man who wud raise 'e han'
On such a' important night, it even harder to undahstan'
Nah Bajan cud accept anyone laying dem han' pon you

Grammy night we all wanted to hear "Barbados this makes," two
Robyn, do like a robin and pick up and fly
And none ah we wud question you, we all undahstan' why
There is a brighter future still ahead wid a lotta happiness
And none o' dis is contingent pun a relationship wid Chris

A Pink Ribbon For Love

A small lump appeared during a loving caress

Panic ensued; I could no longer touch her breast
It was an unbearable thought; that dreaded big C
Now might take her life away from me
Kisses brought tears and soon, a biopsy too

Results confirmed what we already knew
In her young life her mother had died
Breast cancer took her and I watch how my wife cried
Because of this we had been proactive all the while
Only genetics negated our changed in lifestyle
Never was there a chance, we just delayed what would be

Fat free, no alcohol, lots of exercise and mammograms routinely
Our days got edgy when she started the chemo
Radiation therapy brought her to the lowest low

Long days and months and even longer years
Overcame the cancer and dried the tears
Victory came because of our early detection
Ecstasy returned, I didn't lose her to that cancerous intrusion

A Ride In The Park

Around, Ossie rode in the Park and when he came about

Riding without legs on the pedals to his mother he'd shout
I cuh do this mum, look nah feet!
Dear be careful and watch out, don't go in the street
Enjoying it all he returned riding with only one hand

I cuh do this too, look mum, I is a one hand man!
Now be careful, his mum said, but dah is good

Then he went around again and like the boys from the hood
He had both hands off and shouted, look no hands mum!
Even though his mother was troubled she didn't succumb

Pedal around Ossie just one last time
And Ossie took longer and returned off the bicycle with a mime
Ready now dear? But why yah tek sah long and why yah on yah feet?
Kaput was the bicycle, Ossie, in impaired tone said "luk mumma nuh t'eet"

Absolutely Absurd

A long and heavy snow
Barricaded our home with no where to go
So it's the perfect opportunity
Opportunity to show how he missed me
Love had been punctuated with long stays at work
Under all the stress he never once shirked
To stay at home even to mend what we had
Every day he ran off leaving me at home sad
Love was given this gift of snow
Yet my love worked on the computer doing what I didn't know

And then I saw a news reel when comfort I did seek
Booming business brought 2500 new members in a week
Stupid people who have their lovers right there
Using the Internet to seek love elsewhere
Rational thought drew me love's computer to explore what I heard
Darling left the screen up and what I saw was Absolutely Absurd

Accident And Emergency

A recent visit to our local A&E
Cleared my conscience and confirmed my negativity
Chronic sufferers are punished there for being sick
I watched in quiet anguish at this farcical clinic
Doors at the entrance are broken and wouldn't close
Everyone who touches them is contagiously exposed
No protection inside from passing cars' fumes
The cigarette smoke or the pungent perfumes

A single-occupant bathroom is a great health threat
No regular sanitizing has been employed yet
Dangerous people enter and boisterously misbehave

Empathy is foreign to these mentally deprave
Medical attention early was never meted out
Even to those who would in agony shout
Registered nurses were being called away
Got other emergencies remote from A&E that day
Enclosed in a small room with uncomfortable chairs
No hint of a health conscious institution that cares
Could be that there are exceptions but for me
You pay nothing and receive less at our local A&E

And Greater Will Our Nation Grow

A eyeful en' a bellyful", somewhat like "yuh cud look but cahn touch"
Nothing is possessed until it's right in your clutch
Don't hang yuh hat wih yuh hand cahn reach"

Get used to your limits and practice what you preach
Respect due to a dog", and so to any one of us
Everyone regardless to race, gender, religion and status
A pint pot can hold a gill, but a gill cahn hold a pint pot"
There are some situations reversible but some are not
Evah skin-teet en' a laugh" and you will find
Regardless to outward shows all actions are not genuine

When a bird fly too fast he does fly pas' 'e nest"
It is never wise to be overly ambitious, some caution is best
Lime juice cahn spoil vinegar"
Little white fibber can't corrupt the compulsive liar

One smart dead at two smart door"
Unanimously, however ahead of the game you are, there's someone that is more
Relatives should take care of each other, feuding they ought not

Notice Bajans say "Water does run, but blood does clot"
And to warn you of the dangers of your trips to the seashore
The old people would say "De sea ain't got nuh back door"
If black bird fly wid pigeon 'e will get shoot"
Out running with bad company you'll get their treatment how ever big or minute
Now "Yuh cahn be in de church an' de chapel too"

Got to mind your own business, don't get tie up in other people's do
Remember "De devil does find work fuh idle hands to do" each day
One without work soon gets up to mischief and wayward play
We can live by these and other local proverbs we know
Yes we can live positively And Greater Will Our Nation Grow

Another Beautiful Morn

Awoke from a restful night
No sun as yet, no daylight
Outside the dark enveloped about
There was no desire then to go out
Hands clasped as I knelt to pray
Earnestly I thanked the Lord for His new day
Radio kicked in just as I was done

Brought on a newness with the morning sun
Early dew drops sparkled like gem stones
All the drops from flowers still folded like cones
Unusual quiet came across the hill
There was a calm in the air and the leaves were still
I went out to stretch my limbs and inhale the morning air
For a while it felt like I was living elsewhere
Unfortunately I had a very short fantasy
Lots of noises stripped my tranquility

Motorcycles, trucks, cars, buses and more
On this morning it got louder than ever before
Radio hosts on the Morning Show takes me far away
New serenity comes from the music these radio hosts play

Autism

A rising number of kids are falling prey
Unable to be diagnosed with what made them this way
The authorities refuse to accept the theory
It's the vaccinations creating this anomaly
So many kids who may have this illness
May bring great joy and make their families feel blessed

Bajans It is A New Week

Brave the change of this new week
All will be found if you dare to seek
Just ask and you shall receive
And each door you knock on opened if you will believe
No need to doubt
Show a positive attitude and you'll work things out

If you walk, step bravely
Travel by car, travel safely

In life be certain and your choice
Should always be made with a convinced voice

After your decision don't hesitate

Never let second guessing control your fate
Every day is the start of new things
Weeks the signal of these new beginnings

Wake up fellow Bajans to the Cockle Doodle Doo
Every time the Rooster crows, he crows for you
Each time to alert you to get up and get on your way
Keep a positive attitude, God smiles as you kneel and pray

Blind Sight

Blackness all around and the eyes can't perceive
Light as bright as the Sun is as dark as mourners grieve
Incapacity brought on by a body diseased
Neuritis in the Optical left and right and other nerves teased
Don't feel sorry about this for in blindness we can see

Sharpen senses soon heighten perceptibility
In the soul a spirit glows to brighten the day
God's hand guides every step of the way
How great to be blind to the ills of society
To see with the heart and to see God's glory

Blood Test Today

Bajans were in their numbers today
Lots were waiting for what the doctor would say
Overcrowding the room and adjoining corridors
Outside the blood clinic where they exchanged horrors
Didn't hear much, I refused to listen

These strangers chatted until their wait was done
Every time I visit the anticoagulation clinic
Stories of horror visits are shared in it
Time ago I heard of an amputee losing the wrong leg

The old cricketer who now walks with a peg
One patient told of the dangerous overdose
Drug prescription miswritten for another sounding close
All I want is hear them say when they call my name
Your INR is good, your dosage remains the same

Breast Cancer

Best protection is early detection
Reduce your risk by adjusting your lifestyle
Every alcoholic drink will mean cancer risks escalation
And you may reduce your risk by breastfeeding your child
Studies say get physical, walk regularly
Try also to maintain a low fat diet

Careful self checks should be done monthly
And yearly mammograms should become a habit
Never neglect your family's breast cancer history
Communicate this to your doctor as soon as you can
Early prevention if you can but if you can't then detection early
Radically increases your chances to eradicate a cancerous invasion

Call It MS - Marathon Sabbatical

Companies reject you as unfit to work
And staying at home makes you feel berserk
Liability can't be held when you are fired
Laws don't protect your job and few are hired

It's hard to be unproductive and where is your income
The medication is costly and there's home renovations for some

Many still have productive years and work is practical
So the lay offs make me Call It Marathon Sabbatical

Call It MS - Mary Springer

Comically I searched for why, why me
And humorously thought it was hereditary
Looking back and yet not having to look too far
Learnt there was MS in my family in a form bizarre

I know now that it was part of my fate
This MS was there though it appeared late

Mom's name starts with M and surname was S before dad wed her
So I always had MS in my family, I Call It Mary Springer

Call It MS - Mock Sport

Comprising the CNS is the spinal cord and brain
A network of nerves sending impulses like links on a chain
Links made from a sandwich a lipids and protein
Letting impulses leap speedily in between

If there is damaged to the axon links the message gets mix
The sensory nerves send electrical shocks or more subtle tricks

My carpet felt like grit, I walked on hot sand, a CNS misreport
Sensory nerves now play with me so I Call It Mock Sport

Call It MS - More Spiritual

Christ is my Savior but I veered on my way
And neglected to praise Him every day
Life took a change and He drew nigh
Lifted me up as the days went by

I soon found a strength and a radiant spirit
The Lord blessed me with a new sight and a new habit

My days are full of praise, I'm a renewed individual
Since MS changed my lifestyle I Call It More Spiritual

Call It MS - Mostly Scares

Can't predict or calculate with certainty
Any episodes in your MS malady
Looking on to others who'd been diagnosed for years
Lets you see where you might be headed and scares

It supposedly affects everyone differently
Though for most there is an obvious finale

Many worry of the unknown and harbor fears
Seeing MS sufferers I Call It Mostly Scares

Call It MS - Multiple Sclerosis

CAT scans repeated, the add dye in the MRI
And nothing explains why you can't see through one eye
Lumbar test to determine other anomalies
Long stays in hospital but no certainties

It's Acute Disseminated Encephalomyelitis, ALS or even Lyme
The possibilities are great an seem more all the time

Many doctors can't pinpoint and make an accurate diagnosis
So when unsure they default and Call It Multiple Sclerosis

Cat Luck en' Dog Luck

Cindy was promiscuous with a multiplicity of men
And never once got a SDI, STD, an abortion or had children
This girl was attractive and had a body that wouldn't quit

Looked like a movie star and had a tantalizing wit
Ursula was her cousin and the opposite of this
Church life consumed her, that's where she met Chris
Kept virtuous for years, Chris would be the only one

Engaged him, let down her hair and her adventure begun
Now both girls ventured for pleasure bareback

Didn't take precaution but one hid to shun social attack
One girl who remained loyal but took the chance
Got news that woke her from the premarital trance

Like her cousin she had been living in promiscuity
Unlike her cousin, Ursula contracted HIV
Cat luck en' dog luck and like actions may have varied results
Kudos to all who know the rareness of being responsible adults

Cheap Tings Nuh Good

Called me miser and penny pincher
Had your laughs because I didn't squander
Even criticized the quality of what I buy
And labeled me as having a cheapskate eye
Price always mattered for me

Took no consideration for longevity
I think the lower the price the better
Nothing, at whatever cost could last forever
Got some shoes just the other day
Should have seen how much they asked me to pay

Not a cent over the tag of 2.93
Unbelievably priced, I went on a buying spree
Had a revelation when I returned to the hood

Good tings nuh cheap and cheap tings nuh good
One of the shoes tore and revealed my toe
Owning them didn't give me a quid pro quo
Didn't justify buying them however cheap
  Cheap tings nuh good and tings nuh good doan keep

Cigarettes

Clouds of smoke blowing in my face
I can't see, I cough, I'm cramped for space
Got to get fresh air soon or I'll asphyxiate
All the years of exposure, I'm now too late
Recurring, prolonged inhalation of cigarette fumes
Exposure to second hand streams in crowded rooms
The price we pay at the leisure of the inconsiderate
They destroy your health and your solitude violate
Every time you're exposed to these walking chimneys
Say a prayer for healing, protection and deliverance, please!

Culturally Impoverished

Can we teach the youngsters the things we knew
Urban life has made our culture taboo
Lots of the things we knew as little kids
Today are foreign and lifestyle forbids
Using toys they created from scratch
Rollers bikes or wooden 'T' shape coasters with 2 wheels to match
And Gutter perks, sling shots and a branch to stick lick
Lots of them now practice to box and kick
Lots more stay at home with some digital computerize game
You'll never hear Puss Puss catch a corner, so what's our aim?

I miss Black Bitch, Ice Blocks, Bandits and Star Lights
Marbles, playing holes, Dandy Lion Pictures and Flag at nights
People have forgotten how to hop a bus and letting the tarp down
Our Kids didn't even see cane trash lying on the ground
Very few know the smell of the molasses from the plantation
Even fewer tasted cane juice, and call themselves Bajan!
Remember frogs in dozens crossing the roads
In fields butterflies and lady birds out numbering these toads
So much of past Barbados is lost because we
Have these new desires to live in luxury
Eliminate all semblance of life back from then
Don't we want to share Beautiful Barbados with our children?

Cutting Out This Risk

Caesarian section is the method they still teach
Uterine intrusion by abdominal incision releasing babies in breach
This procedure sounds barbaric when we take this route
Taking a baby from its mom by cutting it out
I was crestfallen when I learnt of a young lady's demise
Never waking from her sleep, never opening her eyes
Got ill weeks after the baby was cut from her womb

Opening the doors that led to her early tomb
Ugly opening not healing, across her belly
Threatening and painful, it had become smelly

This lady took lots of pride in her outward show
Her scarring would have been a heavy blow
It may have changed the way she would dress
Such things now seem trivial in her final place of rest

Rudiments in health care should always be
Involve with the total care of patients and especially
Should never be hasty to make the incision
Keep closer watch on patients when we make this decision

De Las' Calf Kill De Cow

David moved quietly
Entered the room discreetly

Looked around to find
Anything that was left behind
Something like the TV from the house next door

Computer or anything to fetch even more
And there before his very eyes
Laid and even greater surprise
Five stacks of hundred dollar bills

Kept in the cupboard behind the pills
It was his easiest theft yet
Lots easier than taking the TV set
Loads of money and nothing to sell

David ran with excitement but tripped and fell
Ended up in the empty pool where he laid unconsciously

Caught later by the neighbors living next door to me
Our district, plagued with theft will be quiet now
We know it'll stop because De Las' Calf Kill The Cow

Disappearing

Do you remember the last time you saw me
I've been disappearing gradually
Started by the year, then by the month and now by the day
A little by little, I've been vanishing away
People who see me are but a chosen few
Possessing special characteristics, an intimacy too
Exceptional closeness which gives them the ability
An insightfulness with each opportunity
Remember my smile that once shone bright
It now spends each day fading 'til night
None but a few will ever see me
Gradually I'm disappearing from society

Expensive Drugs

Every time I see the medication I take
'Xpensive drugs it's a sacrifice I make
Research could be faster and I wish it would too
Every time I take the drugs I get more subdue
Not just the hardship of financial strain
Such unrealistic pricing seem manageable, time and again
It's the knowledge that I give more than I pay
Vast users experience vital organ decay
Essentially the drugs can drain an irreplaceable bounty

Deplete value that is worth more than money
Relapsing remitting Multiple Sclerosis
Usually requires high toxins by diagnosis
Good to delay episodes but sometimes more pay than salaries
Such Expensive Drugs might cost you a liver and kidneys

For Those Ill In Bed

Father, dear Lord this morning I pray
Our family and friends ill in bed may
Rest in your care comfortably

They don't have the energy to get out to see
How beautiful your morning has become
Or smell the daytime, Lord don't let them succumb
Send them the early rooster's crow
Each bird that sings and the sunlight's glow

In bed Father there is much still to enjoy
Let them feel the other beauties that you employ
Like early morning sounds of your people about

Its merriment for others who go out
Night has passed and they have another day

Blessed them with your love that they might say
Each day Lord, thank you for another opportunity
Delight I will Lord in You, my friends and family

God Bends You When You....

Got more to stage management than people realize
On performance nights with the lights in your eyes
Doing your best is not all, you need do more

But if you believe, God's with you, there on the floor
Every time you think you have given your all
No more left, you've done the long haul
Don't give up, there's still more left in your tanks
So believe my brother and give God thanks

You are the vessel through which he works
On your lowest of lows, He pulls you from idle jerks
Uses your faith and converts it to will

Works your body like it has much more still
He bends you when you thought you can bend no more
Energizes you beyond what you've ever been before
Never give up, remember, you're never at the end

You have a more pliable character, with which to bend
On God have faith and in yourself, have faith too
Use this faith and you can perfect anything you choose to do

Hanging Up The Guns

How often I fought to protect my rights
And shot down enemies in daring fights
Never turning away from threats to me
Gunned down the fiercest enemy
I fought and never ran away
Numb sometimes but I chose to stay
Got torn and scarred but I stood up brave

Until wounds from this new enemy were so grave
Pain was different, it was as if new

This enemy hurt in more ways than I knew
How often I fought but now it's easy to quit
Easy to give in to this stealth bandit

Guns seem hopeless against this enemy
Useless to defeat the debility
Now my fight is fought by the spirit within
Such a battle against MS, like all others, I'll fight to win

Honouring His Legacy

How many others follow his style on stage
Or copy his entertainment but never taking a page
Never follow in his philanthropy
Or be as interested in the sick as he used to be
Under the glitz of jewels shone a caring soul
Rhinestones never glittered to show his whole
I saw his soft spirit, his calmness, his love
Not just the iconic musician but a pioneer thereof
Guinness records say he's the most giving, but for me

His life must not be defined as his measured charity
I rather think of the changes that he brought about
Stardom was ingenious but through his clout

Lots of doors got opened to change racial disparity
Entertainers were not judged by skin colour and ethnicity
Giving never stopped even when hard times came
All his life he gave the impoverished the fruit of his fame
CD's, DVD's and others will preserve Michael in time and space
You'll need emulate his giving to "Make this world a better place"

Humility And Patience

Hour after hour and with each one the worst
Unwell Bajans sought healing but needed to wait first
My experience recently at our A&E
Imparted a lesson in patients and their humility
Lots of us who need the instant fix in our lives
In times when trauma or bad health arrives
There is an unnatural tolerance that we will show
You wait impatiently, but more severe cases you let go

And through hours of pain and suffering
Never losing humility for the person who seems dying
During the 12 hours before the doctor saw me

Patients came in and were dispatched with priority
And all the while humbled that there was no choice
There never came a time that I protested with voice
I saw patients helping each other, showing they can care
Even for a stranger whose illness they were unaware
Noticed patients full of patience and humility
Comfortable though their surroundings was misery
Emergency care for disease, illness or accidents
Can enlighten you and awaken Humility And Patience

I Am Learning How to Talk Like A Bajan

I have been reading some Blog entries

And noticing that Bajan dialect is full of anomalies
Many English words carry new meanings

Like Hell a good thing and a weapon called Collins
Every word they emit with nasal sound
And remove harsh letters, that's what I found
Repeats are done for emphasis
None of the Bajans will explain this
I in a word, when should it change to E?
Never knowing which, "ah" or "uh" confuses me
Got a clue from Cheese-on-bread today

Her Blog tries to explain what Bajans say
On Friday she published some of the idiom
Extracts she borrowed from another dot com

This here is my challenge, to use the slang
Objective criticism is welcomed from any of the gang

Tek away mah bread and two then yuh cyaah me on scruffy
And yuh doan mind yuh own business, yuh always too gypsie
Leff me loan and doan off-set me like yuh did before
Keep yah distance coz I aint gun be yuh poppit nah more

Licrish fuh chu you gone and eat all the Jug
I cyant believe you cud come saying "gimme a hug"
Kissing me then yuh skin yuh teet', but never again
Every time it ends up, you just complain

And now I gun go, if yuh miss me I aint dey

But me bozie, I aint gun scotch again, nuh way
Aint getting horn nuh more, nor getting lick up
Juk in the eye, catspraddle and chopped wid nuh teacup

A life at the horsepital even pon a bank holiduh
Now gun stop coz I dunnin wid yuh

I Used To Take It All For Granted

It's a new awakening to a new day

Ushered in by the sounds of the animals as I kneel to pray
Some roosters crowing from the house next door
Eager to awake us all so they crow and crow even more
Darkness slowly walks away

The sunlight creeps out to announce the day
On top of the roof a dove coos its hello

Then the Black birds flock noisily and wouldn't go
A cow in the distance says moo
Kept it up and I never knew
Every moo too was another way to say

It's a good morning and all is okay
Today I'll breathe in God's fresh air

And I'll give Him thanks for the beauty we share
Love of each other and the things around
Like these birds and barn animals, like the dew on the ground

For the day I'll give Him thanks that I can see
Our togetherness and love of community
Radio hosts who starts us right

Getting us off to work in this new day's light
Refrains of old music, Sky watch and their Cock-a-doodle doo Morning Show
All this I once took for granted but I now know
Now I see each day as a blessing with newness and cares
The song says I'm walking on Sunshine and it melts your fears
Excitement all around to let us know it's okay
Doesn't it feel good to walk on Sunshine today!

I Wish You Were...

I was promiscuous and got a child

Was kicked out from home and lived poorly styled
I got another son from the father of my boy
Should've used prophylactics but he said he wouldn't enjoy
He screamed at the children for the slightest thing

Yelled to the top of his voice, unceasing
One night when from a nightmare the children arose
Uncaringly he grabbed a belt ready to share blows

When I stopped him and argument broke out
Everything was my fault, he started to shout
Room after room, he cried out to the kids with blatant scorn
Exclaiming vehemently "I wish you had never been born!"

If I Could Only Talk

I didn't say that
For years it was idle chat

I got on the roof top

Cockle Doodle Doo then I stopped
One human put words to my crow
Unfair words I know
Lots of people are now repeatedly
Discrediting my crowing unfairly

On mornings for years I've tried
No one seems to believe that man had lied
Laughing at my attempts to turn things around
Yet every morning I get up to take the highest ground

Then, at the top of my lungs I crow
And if you listen you too would know
Lies, somebody telling lies about my Cockle Doodle Doo
Keep saying I'm lazy and asking "How could you do so little too"

It's a New Day!

I heard the Rooster crowed at 11:30
There must have been something causing it to crow this early
Sleep hardly came, it was a restless night

And the Cock-a-doodle-doo came again at daylight

Now he must have worked for over pay
Employed to crow at night and the crack of day
Work must be hard but he would proudly

Do his part to ensure I get up early
And he never fails to wake me up and say
You got to get up and enjoy it. It's A New Day!

It's A Perfect Day

I'm off and ready for my morning sea bath
The day started with an enjoyable laugh
Schuster the Rooster reminiscing what happened to Jim

A red rooster that had 16 sexy chickens chasing him

People start their Fridays ready
Excited for the finish to run off and party
Rub the belly pun me, sings one song
Fat men is my preference not the slim and long
Eye candy wrapped in the many ways
Candy flavored any how nowadays
The candy Jim saw running him around the yard

Didn't excite him and he ran and ran hard
As Schuster the Rooster crowed his Cock-a-doodle-doo
You could hear him snickering "Jim died with a smile too!

It's The Right Thing To Do

I've spent the last 24 years of my life trying
To make a difference to children, now one is dying
She has a rare kidney disease threatening her life

The feeling is overwhelming; I'll go under the knife
How often this 13yrs. old felt dizzy and in pain
Eager to dance and play outdoors again

Right now Carla, her mom, says she's lost 85 percent
In kidney functioning so her transplant is urgent
Got this gift of life to give her and hope that she
Have a normal life after the transplant surgery
Told her that from then she'll always have me around

That I'll stick to her like flea on a hound
How I'll donate this kidney from my heart
I'm happy to play this significant part
Now, unquestionably I'll make a difference to a child
Giving this gift brings more that a grateful smile

This gift I pray shall keep on giving
Over and over, a life worth living

Diseased with focal segmental glomerulosclerosis
Overcome it with Principal Friel's kidney, given to Morgan Corliss

Lets Talk Culture

Last chance to see
Eff these things we do is we
There will be discussions where you can say
Something about anything that troubles you today

This is we culture, I always hear
And still I feel like I've been living elsewhere
Look at the streets, they used to be small gaps
Kept stand pipes where people bathe under taps

Cross the road where there was a pasture
Used to play marble cricket and during rains, was one with nature
Lots of neighborhoods where you knew everybody
Transformed, now strangers live in a gated community
Under the tamarind tree where I got chopped
Retailers have a Mall, some classy membership shop
Everything thing I knew as a child, that I thought was Bajan
Some how gone, replaced, so Gabby, this is my Emmerton!

Living As If There Was No Tomorrow

Lulled by the news of my debility
I changed the way I lived drastically
Very restrictive diet and exercising each day
I no longer work or socialize; I'm now a shut away
Nowadays the shroud of uncertainty
Got my lifestyle curtailed and limits me

A lot of things I did with incredible ease
Soon became physical peculiarities

I concentrate just to walk across a room
Fix the monitor to read at a higher zoom

The floor in our house can be hot like tar
Have intermittent bouts like I've been hit by a car
Each day there is something I couldn't predict
Remittent relapses from nerves failing to transmit
Early on mornings I carry on my left side

Weight about 300lbs which hinders my stride
All these things which are bothers to me
Should have caused me to give up and live wastefully

News like this sends tremors far away
Our loved ones are shaken despite what they portray

They may react differently yet feel the same
Or some crawl into a state even therapists can't name
Months he cried then had a change in personality
Obnoxious, withdrawn and it seems he blames me
Regardless to what I do or what I say
Restricting his diet or outlook brings further dismay
Objectionable behavior only came after our sorrow
Why is he **Living As If There Was No Tomorrow**?

Living With MS

Life has changed in many ways
I don't drive or work nowadays
Various chores once easy to do
I now give up trying, I can't see them through
Now, every other day I take a med
Got another one daily before I go to bed

When I'm touched my left side turns to rock
I reduce working with my right hand to avoid electrical shock
There is little coordination from the left hand
Have impaired vision but I understand

Multiple Sclerosis causes the nerves to transmit incorrectly
So I treat it all like they are making Mock Sport with me

Message from the Womb

Mommy and Daddy, cry not for me
Everything would be well in Eternity.
So many days we had and we shared
So many times you showed how much you cared.
All the fun I had on the umbilical swing,
Got cushioned when I fell so I was never bruising.
Enjoyed the rhythms, music and gurgling sound

Frolicked, swam and kicked all day long.
Remember my joy, I never cried
On you I depended and on you I relied.
My meals were regular and always great,

They were never too hot and never came late
How happy I slept in my water bed
Every dream was good when I rest my head.

We had our joy together but now I must go
On a journey I hope you'll come to know.
My Heavenly Father called and on Him I will obey
Be good to each other and remember to pray.

Mind Over Matter

Maybe you'll find this a useful tip
I've taken a saying and made a flip
No pain no gain and mind over matter
Don't even touch what I now capture

Our lives are made up of mind, body and soul
Vying for supremacy in young and old
Exercise strengthens the body but not the mind
Righteousness nourishes the soul and now I find

Mind speaks to soul and body too
A healthy soul tells the mind what the body should do
Told that in weakness God's strength is made perfect
Then the weaker the body the stronger the spirit
Enriching your life by nourishing your soul
Reaps a mind and a body as pure as gold

Multiple Sclerosis

Many people are affected in dissimilar ways
Unique in their afflictions and how they get through the days
Life for many is constantly having to adjust
To changing mobility and whatever else they must
I know of the uncertainties and changes they make
Pain from the easiest of tasks and smiles that are fake
Lots of people who don't understand, can't accept the new you
Everyone prefers the old person they once knew

So they make it harder on you but they don't know
'Cause you never let on, you never let it show
Life now is about being thankful each day
Even for small mercies you would earnestly pray
Running out of the rain or just being able to walk
Or be better able to see peoples' faces when they talk
So many years I took for granted the sensation of touch
I now miss the gentle pleasure of caress so much
Show you care, learn about MS and with Many Share
Let the MS person know you really do care

Multiple Sclerosis - MS (Mock Sport)

Myelin is a white matter coating your nerves
Used by the body it conducts and preserves
Lets impulses run from sensors to brain
They sheath wrap the axons which they contain
I learnt their makeup from a story for kids
Protein layer between two of lipids
Like the rubber that sheaths the electrical wire
Each nerve is protected from the internal weather

Sometimes though the sheath may break
Causing the nerves to not communicate
Losing their messages in midstream
Electrical blackout with conditions extreme
Responses by individuals frequently vary
Often blindness and restricted mobility
Symptoms early in many display
Intense numbness and sometimes may
Send ghost impulses throughout the body

Making you feel like there is some emergency
Only your sanity will cause you to know
Cold bouts or hot patches are all a scam show
Keeping mind over matter is the biggest task

Surviving the attacks with your bravery mask
Pain may tell you it was a heavy roller van
On top of you crushing away on your hand
Reacting nerves get confuse with what to convey
The truths of their garble is revealed when you pray

My Worst Enemy

Multiple Sclerosis is not like anything you know
Your body looks able but it doesn't feel to go

What do you do when you can't move your feet
Or comfortably raise your hands to eat
Red is a color you no longer perceive
Shocking pains dart but you can't believe
There is nothing you can do to make it right

Every doctor says it'll be an eternal fight
None of them giving hope yet no two people are the same
Experiencing MS is like a guessing game
My life was do good, no drugs or alcohol and watch my health
You wouldn't believe my worst enemy turned out to be MySelf

Myasthenia Gravis (MG)

Muscle cells no longer adequately receive
Your impulses which the nerve cells perceive
Attacks are raged by your very own
System responsible for immunity alone
The eyelids may droop and fatigue sets in
Hard to swallow and there's general weakening
Everyday is different but everyday you say
Nothing will spoil this incredible day
Incurable it may be but never compelling
Autoimmune diseases in you need not win

Got to keep on living the life you know
Revel when you can, let the pearly whites show
Accentuate the positive and the negative eliminate
Value great people and the simple ones appreciate
It comes as no real surprise to me
Someone like you conquering this MG

Nothing Yet

No word since the biopsy
One week passed then 2 now 3
The laboratory said they'll be no delay
Have it back for you within a day
I should have known that I could expect
Nothing but mediocrity and disrespect
Going in to them they had little care

Your worst experience, your darkest nightmare
Even though others may have some anxiety
This test result is just a brick in God's Path for me

One Week Starts With But One Day

Once I opened my eyes and turned the radio on
No more lethargy, the laziness was gone
Ears were perked and I started to sway

When I heard the "One" tunes they found to play
Every One as familiar as the One before
Encouraging me to give just a little more
Kept me remembering that the drudgery ahead

Starts with just One step, stepping down from bed
That how ever long it seems, the week starts with but One day
And the load is lightened when I step down to kneel and pray
Radio host announcing happy birthday and anniversary
Those reminders of love shared in family
Schuster the rooster crowing from the top of the trees

Warm sun rising to guide the birds and the bees
I heard of Wanda and Kay
That they'll Dine for One Dollar on their special day
Heard the music saying that You're still the One

Bringing your special remedy to get along
Uniqueness that defines your personality
The special blend that makes you One, gives you individuality

One man with an Audacity of Hope to put the world on track
Now is the President of America, the first Black
Each One cell in the body although micro has a big role

Do your part however remedial, it's essential to control
All the harmony of this universe and with ever day that's begun
You are One love, One Heart, the only One, a vital and special One

Only Ten Men

One Crop-Over I went out to party
No more, the man shouted, we got enough men already
Ladies can go in but as for you men
You were warned before, they're only letting in ten

They closed the gates in my face
Every man outside was barred from the place
No more, from as early as quarter to nine

Men never got a chance to go in to wind
Every woman inside was feeling the blues
None of them dance without taking off their shoes

Organs Donation

Ordinarily you need sign before you die
Releasing your organs for the donors supply
Giving them over to those patients in need
A transplanted organ so operations may proceed
Now many countries are changing their Laws
Shifting the wording of the Donors Clause

Donating will be mandatory unless you otherwise state
On a living will, your unwillingness to donate
Now patients need not wait in a long donors' line
And compatible organs will be easier to find
The availability of organs should greatly increase
Internal transplants, and deaths may decrease
Overtime we'll be a Society of spare parts
Now masking inner beings, if this new Law starts

Ossie Moore and The D's

Outstanding students had to recite
Sentences constructed from words that might
Sometimes give problems so the teacher would insist
Incessant revisions that would consist
Every boy creating sentences of their own

Making the words linked and never standing alone
Ossie Moore got up and the teacher said
One sentence with Deduct, Defense, Detail and Defeat from your head
Remembering what had happened just this morning past
Excitement came, for once he felt like the brightest in class

And he turned around that they all would see
Nothing more than his face smiling in glee
Didn't want the moment to just slip by

Thirty boys before him failed and he was the last to try
He turned to the front to face the teacher again
Eagerly he blurted out his sentence from his brain

De duck that flew over de fence was mine to eat
So I jumped to hold de tail but caught it by de feet

Our Bathsheba

Once the name is spoken
Uttered in circles, emotions are broken
Remembrances of the adultery

By King David contriving when he
Arranged the absence of Uriah the Hittite
That with his wife Bathsheba he might
Have carnal knowledge and do as he may
She had tempted him taking a BATH SHE BAred skin each day
Have our beautiful coast been named after he
Etched in our souls to remind us that we
By the beach have these tempting BATHS HE BArely could withstand
Are we flocking to Bathsheba tempted by her naked sea and sand?

Over Jenkins Walls

Old and Psychiatric people alike
Various mental cases like my uncle Mike
Either willingly or by force were kept
Right behind the green now gray gates where they slept

Jenkins was the name from the community
Everybody knew it by this, where psychiatry
Never was understood and was something to fear
Kept overnight, you will seldom get out of there
I know nuff Bajans were scared
Numbers of people morbidly feared
So when I heard of Ossie going in

Wasn't surprised to hear the escape he was planning
Another inmate told Ossie that come midnight
Leh we climb cross to the other side, he will hold the light
Look, Ossie said, I 'aint walking cross pun dah light beam to dah pad
So dat when I get half ways you cuh turn off the light, yah t'ink I mad

Pan On The Sand

People went out in numbers this weekend
A family show or a show suited to take a friend
No disturbances recorded, the Police said

One of the best shows ever, its popularity will spread
Now I didn't go but from what I hear

There is much regrets if you too weren't there
Having an evening with Pan music and the sand on your feet
Edwin brought out lots of youngsters and they too had a treat

Samuel Jackman Polytechnic should start making pans
And music camps structured to suit their fans
Not traditional arrangements but those pan players who know
Developing this music needs presentation and funds to grow

Patience

Please have patience patients we'll get to you
All resources are employed to see that we do
Though your wait seems long in an uncomfortable chair
It's the best we have and we are doing our best in here
Even when it appears you're having an unnecessary delay
Nurses are doing everything to these problems allay
Care is taken to ensure thoroughness and accuracy
Every measure is taken to encourage your treatment promptly

Patients

Patience patients, he will soon be here
And stay in you chair, don't go anywhere
The Doctor is on the ward making a call
It shouldn't take long, we were told, not at all
Emergencies will happen, you've been there before
Nurses over your bed, hoping the doctor could do more
The health cycle is vicious but it always starts with you
So patience patients, you'll soon see Dr. Karoo

Patients' Patience

People sometimes show strange generosity
At times when you least expect this oddity
They say Sir, Madam, please, excuse me and thank you
In times when they were waiting there for hours too
Emergency rooms are different but in the clinic
No one seems pressured with uncertainty or panic
They willingly exchange deep concern
Show empathy with intimacy they soon will learn

Placed in a hot room with no where to sit
All the patients took to the corridors out of habit
They used chairs from the rooms nearby
I stood for 30mins before I was offered one by a guy
Eventually I learnt of his diseased heart
Noticed a lady who if she could stand, from hers would part
Cancers, diabetes and heart disorders may afflict their bodies
Even after 4 uncomfortable hours they kept polite faculties

Please Take Your Time To ...

Praise God for the weather that He will command
Learn to take your time to work the land
Each word should flow slowly, emphasis strong and not weak
As you present yourself, take your time to speak
Stay in control as you commute, stay alive
Each day you rush, take your time to drive

There is much around, take your time to observe creation
All the plants, the animals, all the people of your nation
Keep your composure, avoid quarrels and strife
Encourage positive thoughts, take your time to enjoy life

You should take bites meticulously, savor the sweet
Once you have been served a dish, take your time to eat
Use time to recover that you might be your best
Relax on those days off, take your time to rest

There is lots to go around, share your delight and cheer
In all you do remember take your time to share
Mankind is given this blessing from above
Embrace a lover and take your time to make love

These are just a few things you encounter each day
On quiet and peaceful time, Take Your Time To pray

Pronunciations

People will sometimes vary
R added places where there shouldn't be
Obama's name is Barack and not the Barrack I often hear
Nation paper even printed Barrack on his inauguration last year
Usually I tolerate slight discrepancies
Not like when people add a "n" to names like De-nise
Calling De-nis, Den-nis is bad and the other way around
I find it hard to hear these without feeling my world upside down
And recently I heard a pro Sports Broadcaster from ESPN
Trashing the pronunciation of Safina, as Sah-fin-nah, so then
I wrote them, got no change; but our own Martin Parris knew
One must say Sah-fee-nuh, he sounded like he had a clue
Now if only I could get people saying Bah-rahk
Sounding as sweetly as Michelle, I wouldn't feel so out of whack

Prostate Cancer

Pain when urinating or the stream getting slow
Rectal examination by a doctor can put you in the know
Or you may have a blood test for your PSA
Such a test done early will also say
That Prostate Cancer is very suspect
A simple blood test or digital test can check
Treatment if caught early can be surgery
Eliminate the metastasis by removing the tumor early

Cancer unattended spreads beyond control
At its first sign let the doctor play his role
Nowadays it's easy, there is little to fear
Careful test after age 40 can be done every year
Early detection greatly reduces the danger
Rids us of the fear and the menaces of Prostate Cancer

Prostate Cayan Sah

Please Father, my friend today
Rests while the doctors cut away
Operating to remove a tumor that's localized
So Father be there as he opens his eyes
This servant of yours, has been good to me
And by all accounts to everybody
Though I scarcely see him between the years
Each time I do, he shows how much he cares

Cancer of the Prostate can be hard to fight
And may creep up upon you like a thief in the night
You get little warning and usually, only when it has done
All the harm to ensure its battle has been won
Not this time though dear Father, you knocked on his door

Signaled him with your message so he may act before
And now I'm sworn to secrecy as they remove his tumor
Hush he told me, so if asked about the cancer, I cayan sah

PTSD - Post Traumatic Stress Disorders

Patriotic men and women who fought with loyalty
Overseas to preserve a country's sovereignty
Soldiers returned home but unaware
The country they fought for will show little care
They battled different races, of many enemies
Raided the terrorists from many countries
And never expected battles to be on homeland
Unable to live productively how others can
Memories and nightmares invade their sleep
And moments that trigger recalls, cause them to weep
They are misunderstood and taunted as being mad
In the streets discarded despite the tours they had
Cast out by society, can't even get work

So they roam the streets as perils lurk
The number of suicides exceed war casualties
Rewards for their bravery is now fatalities
Even though it's noticed by the government of the USA
Such mistreatment of the Vets isn't going away
Some of the soldiers on the outside look strong

Don't look as though there could be anything wrong
It's easy to call them hard back men
So easy to overlook their insidious ruin
Our societies force these men into crime
Risking now for food to eat; caught, they're forced to do time
Don't we see the irony of putting them in jail
Every one we do is another time we fail
Rather than the 40,000 to incarcerate
Soldiers can be cared for in society until they rehabilitate

Puff Legs And Bloomer

People back in the 60's
Used to wear the exposing minis
Fellows loved watching these skirts
Fuse fellows and skirts we got flirts
Legs were shown high above the knee
Every school girl displayed theirs' compulsory
Girls had little choice, it was the trend
So wearing puff legs and bloomer were their conservative mend

A far cry from G-strings and T backs
Nowadays botty riders and others that expose the max
Don't make a comparison about what we wore

Back in the days we couldn't find skimpy wear at any store
Ladies showed their legs but you can believe me
Our derrières were well covered beneath the ominous mini
Once the fashion passed we were glad to get long
Many girls never thought below the knee felt wrong
Eff I wuz a young gal I would cover up all my body
Realizing now that's what gives men the real ecstasy

Recovery

Righteous and Almighty God you ask that we
Exalt your name, give praise, thanks and live uprightly
Comfort my "sister" because it has been her choice
On you she has depended and for you she'll rejoice
Victory you said comes when we first seek you out
Every day she has lived your way as she moved about
Remembering Psalm 27 and what the very first verse said
You're "the strength of my life; of whom shall I be afraid?"

RPB- Rivalry Perpetuates Buddies

Red Plastic Bag and John King
Involved in some healthy rivaling
Vied against each other for years
And now they're true Calypsonian peers
Lyrical geniuses and rear artistes
RPB and John improve on every release
You know Something's Happening when the Bag gets on stage

People feel a piece of Heaven since Johnny Ma Boy got of age
Entertainment extraordinaire, any one
Ready for great things in performance and song
Plastic Bag is a favorite but we must wait
Every indication shows this competition will be great
Can't stop the music all you try
This is our heritage, bear and comply
Under the drum beats the horns and the pan
A Bajan will be hypnotized from the Kaiso band
They will catch you by the feet and make you move
Engulf your spirit and put you in the grove
Some Bajans are hopeless with the Kaiso beat

Bemused by its magic, they will wuk-up in the street
Under the spell they'll do strange things with a stranger
Do this and never worry about ramifications later
Dancing to the Kaiso puts you in hypnotic glory
It's euphoric and with the right artistry
Entertainers Red Plastic Bag and John King
Something's Happening and Heaven might be coming!

Sick

So Father, why am I worrying, what can I do?
I have no dominion on this, so I'm leaving it all to you
Cleanse my body and make it well some day
Keep me comforted during this illness dear Lord I pray

Something's Happening

So many people in the street
One thing controlling their feet
Mass chaos is in the air
Exploding our atmosphere
There are adults and children too
How many people, no one knew
I see trampling as the people scurry
Nobody is stopping to worry
Getting away is first on their mind
'cause staying seems to threaten mankind
Soon above the noise, a loud burst

Hurrying got more but not without some screams first
And then suddenly
People, we could see
Panicking, shouting, "Gun!" It was gun shots
Eagerly, some people with little red spots
Not hurt, but splashed with blood spray
It was a dark, brutal day
Nothing like this has ever happened before
Gunshots tormented the city just at a quarter past four

Stepping Down

So often it is harder than you might think
Taking those first steps without a blink
Each step gets easier but the trouble is with the first
Putting ones foot down is always the worst
People didn't leave the burning roof though the ladder was there
I read Peter didn't disembark because, waters beckoned beware
Noises suspect, so you didn't descend the stairs in the dark room
Giving up a position to youth spells your eventual doom

Didn't take that step down until the bus had stopped
Once you stepped onto the platform your courage dropped
When I was young, for all these occasions I'd jump instead
Now I'm even cautious when I Stepping Down from bed

Stop HIV and AIDS

Sometimes a woman can spread the virus early
Through breast feeding her new neonatal baby
Or people through their sexual transgression
Practice risky behavior and may pass this infection

He and he behavior is not at all alone
It's more risky but there are others the records have shown
Viruses are sturdy organisms and HIV is more so

Any bodily fluid they may enter and in numbers may grow
Normally they'll invade the cells and destroy your immunity
Deficient Immune Systems can't fight even the simplest infirmity
AIDS - Acquired Immunity Deficiency Syndrome
Is a threat to humanity and can afflict any home
Do all you can to fight this mortal enemy
Stop HIV and AIDS from spreading, live responsibly

Talk About It, Let It Stop!

Tears come to my eyes
And mom never acts surprise
Letting her rollercoaster of men
Keep abusing me all over again

All because they pay our bills
Boyfriends of hers take their pleasured fills
Out on me and it hurts, I feel bruised
Used for their convenience, fully abused
Tears come and on my cheeks they dry

I can't scream out loud if even I try
These nightly visits have turned me into a shell

Left me emotionless and created my Hell
Evil has surged into my life
Trusted into me like an assailants knife

I am wounded but mommy doesn't care
Tonight she sent a man in here

She pretended that she was fast asleep
Then he came in and the evil trusted in deep
On the radio I heard of some who cared at Paredos
Parent Education for Development In Barbados

Technology

There is a Kaiso I'm yet to hear
Everyone keeps saying it's the best this year
Could understand why, if it was about technology
How often we trade in, know how, for dependency
Notice we are complaining about TV breaks
Organization and timing is all that it takes
Lots of people now handicapped without their cell
Organization and timing and fewer will sell
Got to hear this song which has so much to address
You and I are far too dependent on technological progress

The Arts Class

Teacher told them draw something fast
He was running out of time, the hour was soon past
Every child quickly gave of their best

A boy drew sailors on a boat another, a policeman in bullets proof vest
Reindeer in a field was one boy's offering
This other drew a teacher lashing a student who was painfully crying
So many action pack drawings they made in the last half of class

Canons on the warzone of one, another a lad courting his lass
Let me see what you have done, the teacher said to Ossie
And he approached the teacher's desk very slowly
So what is this? The teacher asked sternly, just a blank page and a dot!
Sir dah is a 'plane that tek off fast at the airport. You cuh still see it or not?

The Birthday Party

This fellow was stumbling outside a rum shop
He was drunk and disorderly and Ossie begged him to stop
Everyone else out there was cheering him on

But Ossie was not amused and wanted them gone
It was the fellow's birthday and he wanted to celebrate
Rum and coke was the cheapest drink and it tasted great
They encouraged the fellow with an old Irish song
He enjoyed the attention and with them sung along
Do wid a drunken sailor, what do yah do?
And then he told Ossie , now you join in too
Young chap, tell me, how old do you think I am today

Proud he appears younger, he was shock by what Ossie had to say
And how you manage' to guest correct that I was 48
Real easy sir, cause uh de ruckusness you does create
Tek my bruddah, sometimes he is a real nut
Yah see I figuh my bruddah is 24 and he is half-uh-idiot!

The Creator

These gifts Lord they don't understand
How quickly we create upon command?
Every time you speak Lord through my pen

Creating these poems, they ask me Lord, when?
Right away Lord I know, you speak to me
Every time I ask, you're there - free
All I need do is to open my heart
Then you Lord show me where to start
Open my heart and the words pour out
Righteousness and trust leave no room for doubt

The Cure Is Pregnancy

The research I did revealed a startling thing
How pregnancy can cure me from my suffering
Endocrinologists and neurologists never told this to me

Can't believe there is such a natural remedy
Unless they were worried about my age
Ridiculous if they think I'm at the hopeless stage
Elders have had children and they were much older than me

I am by comparison still in my infancy
So why wouldn't they have told me this likely cure

Putting me through tests and drugs, making me impure
Returning to them regularly for more tests
Every month the same grueling physical stress
Got my doubts about their sincerity
No one can tell me they weren't hiding this from me
All the while I could have been in bed
Not sleeping, working on the cure instead
Could have tried this therapy repeatedly
Young ladies could have been pregnant with my baby

The Devious Head Cold

There is a fact scarcely known
Head colds have a motive of their own
Eclipsed by sniffles and fevers is a more hidden sign

Deviously raging their turmoil behind
Every head cold doesn't have this dreaded clout
Veiled by regular symptoms to take you out
It's unsure which ones will eventually be
Onerously wielding this tenacity
Untreated they all have a better chance
Such head colds are dangerously enhance'

Had the misfortune to meet one with exceptional ability
Endowed with the skills of migratory
And two weeks after the head cold is gone
Devious work starts and the worries are now on

CAT scans, Spinal Taps, MRIs and later EEGs
Often will detect problems in the immunities
Learning now that an Autoimmune Disease Is similarly started
Don't let your head cold, however slight, go untreated

The Dining Table

The wedding was over and the honeymoon done
He now had to get the house furniture, one by one
Every thing was paid down for at the department store

Didn't have enough money left back to pay for anything more
In the afternoon a friend brought a donkey cart
Now Ossie's wife told him from the very start
I want tah see everything home when I get there
No stopping by friends, mek sure yah bring the table and armchair
Growing wearier by the minute, it was getting late

Tired Ossie took up everything and left the table at the store gate
And he rushed across the pasture, barely beating his wife to it
But Ossie, she exclaimed, my table 'aint get here yet!
Love don' tell me I rush fah nuttin', stump mah toe, it cahn be true
Eff I did know, I cuddah walk slow, dah table got four legs, I only got two

The Emergency

The relapse came and her body shook
Had no relief from medication she took
Emergency team worked busily together

Everyone pitching in and they sedated her
Mid-afternoon call came and there was much uncertainty
Elusive symptoms leaned towards neurology
Roger told us her convulsions had stopped
Got in contact with their last consulting Doc
Encouraged to see him on December 21st
Now Tani was to wait unless things got worse
Can't understand why wait, why the doctors couldn't today
You'd think from her distress, the 21st was too far away

The Fire Was A Blast!

They piled on their licks and added the kerosene
Hauled out dirty linen and sent KB Kleen
Entertainers stopped by to watch the flames

Fans and friends called in and some people called and left no names
Invited guests were there, seated around the bond fire
Riveting presentations and speeches and colorful attire
Evenings the airwaves lit up with the fireworks

Winks of approval from passersby and some made smirks
And the Mighty Gabby for the first time on air
Shared an unknown gem that was replayed when he wasn't there

A Cocky Commentator added his own sparks

Brought heated discussions to engage like legal sharks
Listeners, you made the flames burned bright
And sharing this with you was a cherished delight
Sorry the Fireworks are out and the flames are now past
This time with you was great and **The Fire Was A Blast**!

The Key To Everything

Time had passed and Ossie got his own place
He bought every new thingamabob and adorned every space
Electric iron, radiogram, blender machine and a color TV

Kept up with the Joneses and gained popularity
Every Tom, Dick and Harry knew him by name
You could hear shouts for Ossie wherever he came

The guys at work never went home at him but knew where he lived
Ossie had adorn the house with flashing lights that would give

Everyone seeing it a lasting memory
Very bright flashes lit the house like a Christmas tree
Early one morning sirens were blurring as fire trucks stormed by
Radio broadcast described a fire gutting a home and no water supply
You hear that Ossie? a co-worker asked with concern
The people described a fire sounding like at his house "evahting cud burn"
He asked Ossie, dah is you house, duh say it did pon a hill top
It have in lots of equipment and it burning nonstop
Nervously Ossie dug into his handbag, then fell to his knees
Goodness mercy! I did scared fah a minute dey, but it cahn be me,
I got my house keys!

The New Normal

The things I took for granted and found easy to do
Have become challenges and impossible too
Exercising regularly brings subtle change

Normal fitness for me now falls in a lower range
Every time I'm asked how do you do
When I'm met by folks who never knew

Nothing I can tell them will ever convey
Onerous challenges I have each day
Remission in health are common for me
My illness is quiet and can move around sneakily
At times I feel better and some days even more
Later that day I might feel worse than days before

The Outpatients

They sit in discomfort and wait patiently
Hours pass and still they sit tolerantly
Exchanging experiences with apparent strangers

Offering comforts to sooth ailing sufferers
Urgency seems foreign to the caregivers there
They move around as if they haven't a care
Patients are all given the same appointment
Arriving early does not prevent disappointment
Time comes and it's your turn to go in
It takes just a few minutes after all the waiting
Each trip to the Outpatients Clinic is the same
Not even after many years do they know your name
The records are archaic and if they are not there
Seeing the doctor on that day would be very rare

The Proposition

The night was going great
He had taken out his sweetheart on a date
Everything was going according to plan

People had been telling Ossie to be a real man
Right after dinner it was already dark
Ossie offered to walk her home through the park
Politely she asked him, "You wannah come in?"
Ossie blushed, nodded fast and gasped like he was outtah win'
She got up from the sofa later and went in her bedroom
In a flash had on skimpy lingerie and expensive perfume
Then called Ossie who slowly went and saw her outstretched on the bed
I want yah tek wah evah yah want Ossie , she said
Ossie dash fah the scissors and hope it would work
Nip and cut 'way all elastic and said, good, I wan'uh mek a gutterperk

The Reason You Rush

Take great care friend, the road too
Has others who wish to get there, just like you
Emergencies can easily follow your incongruities

Recklessness, road rage, drunken driving, any of these
Every time you feel to rush remember that you
Are exposing others to danger too
Slow down dear friend, it's better you be late
One wrong turn of the wheel and you can't keep your date
No schedule you'd made wants to be without you

Your presence is required and those on the road too
Our highways have become the final spot for too many
Unusual accidents happening, untimely

Rushing has been the cause of many of these
Use greater caution when you traverse our highways please
Sitting at the meeting or dining table they wait in calm hush
Have care, Drive to Stay alive; to arrive is **The Reason You Rush**

The Sciences In The Jars

Teacher had a special experiment that day
He brought four jars and held four worms at bay
Experiments were customary but none were like this

Science was suddenly taking a pleasing twist
Come young scientists, he said, observe with me
I have placed mud in jar 4 and in jars 1 to 3
Ethanol in the first, smoke in the second and sperm in the third
Now you can all repeat for me what you have just heard
Class in unison were able to say
Everyone was paying attention that day
So the teacher said here is what I will do

I'll place a worm in each of 1 to 3 and in the 4th jar too
Now I will cover them and overnight they will stay

Then we'll see what happens when we return in one day
He left them there and the class was dismissed
Everyone returned and observed and here is the gist

Jars 1 to 3 the worms died but not in jar 4
And the teacher looked around the class and stopped at Ossie Moore
Right Ossie what do you deduce, speak in your own terms
Sir "As long as ya drink, smoke, and have sex, ya won't have nuh worms!"

The Street Light

The police came and saw Ossie
He stalled for a while to see what he would see
Evening was long gone and it was a dark night

Searching with his head down, Ossie was under the street light
Took almost an hour and still the same
Relentlessly Ossie searched with no shame
Every stone he turned under the light
Even lift up the garbage bin that was in clear sight
The police thought he had seen

Loitering masqueraded and that he had been
In view long enough for the assailant to stop
Gimme a chance sir, I was all the way up dey and some money drop'
He asked Ossie, so why aren't you looking up dey
This sir is obvious, yah cuh see bettah wid de street light down hey

The Teachers' Professional Day

Today they are grown
Have families of their own
Earned a decent life

They strayed from bullying with stick and knife
Education was their eventual choice
And I am glad they found their own voice
Creative in their own ways
Have beautiful things they do nowadays
Educating others too
Right from wrong, the things to do
So now when I look around

Purposed for the origin, I've found
Roosters have much in common with me
One life long ago I started students you see
For years I woke them up in class
Even crowed my disciplines repeatedly until it last
Students need a proper start each day
Schuster the rooster got the right idea
I've heard the nuisance of the musical car horn
Or annoying ring tones on phones in the morn
No sound can be better that from nature's clock
A start in the morning by the Cockle Doodle cock
Life separates people into one of its categories

Don't like waves crushing or the birds and the bees?
And didn't like your teachers either but where are you now
Your mornings are miserable and you never do the things you vow

The Third Miscarriage

The Doctor heard what she had to say
He directed her to come the following day
Evening came, then night, then came the pain

The bleeding did also come back again.
Her husband rushed her to the emergency
In distress they learnt they had lost the baby
Right at the start of the second trimester
Disillusioned if she was destine to ever

Mother a child through natural birth
Impatient to prove her womanly worth
She insisted and wanted her husband to be
Cooperative in causing a new pregnancy
And pressured him into an ultimatum
Reciprocate or she'll be staying at her mum
Running away from emotions wouldn't repair
Intense feelings they used to share
And not understanding his emotional strain
Got to be selfish and ignores his pain
Exempt diagnosis, unwilling spouse, what ever may
Miscarriage showed its face in another way

This Great Morning

The morning was very warm but overcast
Had another good night's rest but now the rest has passed
I awoke to the songs on the radio
Saluting the Ladies of the Caribbean on the Morning Show

Giving praises to the Island Women wherever they are
Riveting local contributions worthy of shores afar
Ethel the Rooster, well not quite his name
A rooster with such a name might crow in shame
They still have to go back to the drawing board but today when

My Cockle doodle doo friend crows, he's crowing for every Caribbean hen
On this day he too celebrates
Rooster knows and like us, participates
No lady goes unnoticed or is forgotten
I see the elderly ladies walking in their garbs of cotton
Noticed some in their gardens and others by the bus stop
God's blessings to you from us and the rooster on the roof top

This Little Piglet

The breeding sow, the pig he cared for had got 14 piglets
He had been given strict instructions that they weren't his pets
In the mornings he was told to bring the sow feed
So he worked hard cutting it grass and some hog weed

Life for him though hectic was rewarding
I heard of his devotion to his chores every morning
Then his mother told him he must make a count
The piglets were all over the yard but he would check the amount
Like clock work he did and all was well
Everyday he counted and everyday he would tell

Put his stool down and waited at milking time and shouted 1, 2, 3
It was that one morning when he stopped at 13 that alarmed me
Got his mother worried too, she shouted praedial larceny call the cops
Loudly she screamed to lift the roof tops
Enraged she confirm with Ossie, you only count 13, boy wha we gun do
This little piglet in de yard wont cum and lemme count he too!

Today's Health- Darkness

There was darkness when I stepped down from bed
Our lights were out so I lit a candle instead
Darkness was parted with my every step
And I was grateful I had candles where I slept
Yesterday I was weak and feeling bad
Some darkness came over me but I also had

His light to go with me through this darkened day
Every step I took with him the darkness was parted away
And I was grateful I had my Savior's light
Lighting my path and giving me sight
Today I'm better and basking in His glory
He washed away my darkness and made me a better me

Today's Health - Forgot My Tablet

Took one tablet this morning as I always do
On evenings as diagnosed I take two
Didn't remember the one yesterday
And didn't double it up today
You mustn't take too high a dosage
Seizures may be brought on from sudden increase usage

How then do you counteract the drop
Emotionally you might think your support will stop
And when you wake up feeling this way
Looks like you'll be having a bad day
Today your body feels weak and broken
Have faith He reminds me, for your Lord has spoken

What A Wonderful World It Would Be

Who dares to deny
How we can be, you and I
A frown replaced with a smile
That lasts more than just a while

A different life

What a wonderful world for man and wife
Or just two friends
Now life transcends
Dare you to prevent
Every joy the Lord has sent
Refuse the morning sun
Forego to laugh while others have fun
Use this day
Let it start this way

When something is wrong
Or you and yours don't get along
Raise your hands to embrace
Let them see a smile on your face
Don't give up my friend, try

It gets easier by and by
Then all will see from here or above

Where is the love
Or when you hear the Cockle Doodle Doo
Ushering in the mornings for you
Listen and you will find
Discoveries that please the mind

Beautiful sights follow the call
Enjoy why the morning is loved by us all

What Chance

What is the chance that she could now
Have this illusive disease somehow
And what is the chance that through one test
They could say with accurate diagnosis

Chances are they would need collaborate
Have more specialist doctors investigate
And even then I'll challenge what I heard
Never giving these medical people the last word
'Cause the Lord alone knows what inflicts us
Even though the doctors may diagnose it as Lupus

What's In A Name

We call him dad or sometimes daddy
He is called by some pop or pappy
And in the third person, my father or the old man
They call him sometimes what ever they can
So many names for someone who is the same

I wonder then of the old TV series that sought to proclaim
No matter how we refer to the creator in Heaven above

A name is but a name once we refer to Him with love

Names in our Christian bible alone are over 20
And we still know each of them refers to the Almighty
Maybe like "The Long Search" proclaimed, we are climbers seeking the top
Every climber a religion, using different tools but heading still to Pop

When I Awoke

My night was good now morning broke
Yawned and stretched when I awoke

Right arm seemed lazy and wouldn't swing
I couldn't control what it was doing
Got overwhelmed when I sat to eat
Had help with my tray and to my seat
Then a blow pierced my reality

How many people go through this daily?
A lost in the use of my dominant hand
Now made me fully understand
Disability comes like the dream you dread

Overnight when you lay secure in bed
Viciously snatching functionality away
Exerting discomfort and causing dismay
Reactions differed when they learnt what I had

Some people believe it was from living bad
Living each day without plenty of rest
Eating poorly and working in stress
People don't know how bless it is for me
This morning I awoke with my entire faculty

Who's My True Ancestor?

When I was young they told me
How my paternal great granddad was an ecky-becky
On my mothers side I had an Indian great grand
She married a half breed Chinese man

My name was taken from an American Lord
Yankee man who travelled by ship with slaves aboard

They said he was originally from Scotland and crossed
Regularly from coast to coast selling men at minimal cost
Under the many gene pools that tainted my blood
East to West, all kinds of manhood

Am I to contend that from my dark colored skin
None of these races have any part within
Can it be that I am chiefly a Black
Ethnically linked to a more African track
Should I refuse the many other tributaries
That converge to form this present man from the West Indies
Or can we not be so devoted to race but rather to blood
Race divides us humanity unites us so which do you think I should?

Yah Hear Dis One 'Bout Ossie

Yeah I tell yah dah is the sun
And I say you are wrong, we better run
How do you expect to see the sun when we were here long after noon

Had hours of drinks in there, that's got to be the moon
Every body knows the sun is up dey
And they also know that's where the moon does stay
Right but de moon dus neveh come out dis early

Don't fool yourself, the moon gets up earlier than we
I once went to the beach and in the blue skies
Saw the moon big and full, couldn't believe my eyes

On that day the sun shone to the left, the moon to the right
Night had long gone, it was day light
Eyes can deceive yah man regularly

But I can't afford to let them deceive me
Once the two men got to a bus stop
Uh gun ask dah man dey that using the pole as he prop
Then they approached the man very slowly

Ossie was by this bus stop and had looked mannerly
Skipper, we want you to settle this
See dah thing up dey in the sky, wah is dah, tell Chris
I wish I knew, that I might settle your despair
Either the moon or the sun but sorry, I don't live down here!

You is ah Bajan?

You would never believe how often they ask me
Of my seemingly elusive nationality
Unsure that I could ever be a Barbadian

Inconsistently pronouncing their cherish Bajan
So often when I'm with a friend in public

And trying to sound like a Bajan chic
How clumsy I poor out my indigenous slang

Butchering this already butchered Lang
And because I speak with an uncertain accent
Just a touch of English, German, French and Spanish decent
All my enunciations are suspect to the Bajan's ear
No one believes I was born and bred here

Your Breath of Fresh Air

Tightening in the chest and its hard to breathe
Her morning didn't take the change she had believed
Early when she got up she felt the pain

After the night's rest she was heavily breathing
She had been here before but couldn't remember
This pain was tightened and burned unlike any other
Her speech got labored and her panting got great
Managing to go work is a risk she couldn't take
A better bet was to get to her doctor's early
There was one is the neighborhood that she could see
It's like deep sea diving and running out of air
Catching for more, inhaling hard but there is none there

And the surface is high and the light you can see
There is a sparkle which shines and offers delivery
The doctor is your hope but he is hours away
And yet there is immediate deliverance when we choose to pray
Coughs, colds, congestions, chronics and cancers He will Claire
Keep focus on Him and He will be your breath of fresh air

About the Author

Khaidji (pronounced KayGee or simply KG) is a Bajan writer who artistically crafts simple words into unusual nostalgic acrostics, with uniquely styled Rhyming Poetry.

When Khaidji was first diagnosed with Multiple Sclerosis it was impossible to write and read since the nerves in the eyes were badly affected and those in the hands were weakened. Over time some sight was restored and greater ease in mobility in the hands and legs. Khaidji's voice is still on and off but the poetry has lent a new voice and rare perspective.

In April of 2009, Khaidji delivered by third party, a signed copy of "Path To The White House" to President Barack Obama. This book had been completed the day after the President's appointed, on November 5, 2008, ready in time for the inauguration.

The acrostics receive very high praise from choice circles and some have been published on international blogs at CNN, MSNBC, Fox News, The Huffington Post and local Blogs like Boyce Voice, Barbados Free Press, Cheese-On-Bread. Many have been read on Radio, with a record 16 being recorded and played on Independence Day, 2009, throughout the day.

This collection of poems is intended to appeal to a wide audience and especially targeted to Bajans. A small few of the poems included here make very specific references and would better be understood with a knowledge of the circumstances for the inspiration. However, an absent of knowledge of these specifics would not reduce the clarity of the style. Khaidji's crafty skill makes the poems entertainment for even the not so avid readers and enthusiasts alike.

www.ingramcontent.com/pod-product-compliance
Ingram Content Group UK Ltd.
Pitfield, Milton Keynes, MK11 3LW, UK
UKHW041937190726
13854UKWH00004B/1640

9 781365 291586